**rockschool**®

# Bass Grade 4

*Performance pieces, technical exercises and in-depth guidance
for Rockschool examinations*

# Acknowledgements

Published by Rockschool Ltd. © 2012
Catalogue Number RSK051214
ISBN: 978-1-908920-13-3

**AUDIO**
Recorded at Fisher Lane Studios
Produced and engineered by Nick Davis
Assistant engineer and Pro Tools operator Mark Binge
Mixed and mastered at Langlei Studios
Mixing and additional editing by Duncan Jordan
Supporting Tests recorded by Duncan Jordan and Kit Morgan
Mastered by Duncan Jordan
Executive producers: James Uings, Jeremy Ward and Noam Lederman

**MUSICIANS**
James Arben, Joe Bennett, Jason Bowld, Larry Carlton, Stuart Clayton, Andy Crompton, Neel Dhorajiwala, Fergus Gerrand,
Charlie Griffiths, Felipe Karam, Kishon Khan, Noam Lederman, DJ Harry Love, Dave Marks, Kit Morgan, Jon Musgrave,
Jake Painter, Richard Pardy, Ross Stanley, Stuart Ryan, Carl Sterling, Henry Thomas, Camilo Tirado, Simon Troup,
James Uings, Steve Walker, Chris Webster, Norton York, Nir Z

**PUBLISHING**
Fact Files written by Stuart Clayton
Walkthroughs written by Stuart Clayton
Music engraving and book layout by Simon Troup and Jennie Troup of Digital Music Art
Proof and copy editing by Stuart Clayton, Claire Davies, Stephen Lawson, Simon Pitt and James Uings
Publishing administration by Caroline Uings
Cover design by Philip Millard

**SYLLABUS**
Syllabus director: Jeremy Ward
Instrumental specialists: Stuart Clayton, Noam Lederman and James Uings
Special thanks to: Brad Fuller and Georg Voros

**SPONSORSHIP**
Noam Lederman plays Mapex Drums, PAISTE cymbals and uses Vic Firth Sticks
Rockschool would like to thank the following companies for donating instruments used in the cover artwork

**PRINTING**
Printed and bound in the United Kingdom by Caligraving Ltd
CDs manufactured in the European Union by Software Logistics

**DISTRIBUTION**
Exclusive Distributors: Music Sales Ltd

**CONTACTING ROCKSCHOOL**
*www.rockschool.co.uk*
Telephone: +44 (0)845 460 4747
Fax: +44 (0)845 460 1960

# Table of Contents

## Introductions & Information

## Rockschool Grade Pieces

## Technical Exercises

## Supporting Tests

## Additional Information

# Welcome to Rockschool Bass Grade 4

## Welcome to Bass Grade 4

Welcome to the Rockschool Bass Grade 4 pack. This book and CD contain everything you need to play bass at this grade. In this book you will find the exam scores in both standard bass notation and TAB. The CD has full stereo mixes of each tune, backing tracks to play along to for practice, and spoken two bar count-ins to both the full mixes and the backing track versions of each of the songs.

## Bass Exams

For each grade you have the option of taking one of two different types of examination:

- **Grade Exam:** a Grade Exam is a mixture of music performances, technical work and tests. You prepare three pieces (two of which may be Free Choice Pieces) and the contents of the Technical Exercise section. This accounts for 75% of the exam marks. The other 25% consists of: *either* a Sight Reading *or* an Improvisation & Interpretation test (10%), a pair of instrument specific Ear Tests (10%), and finally you will be asked five General Musicianship Questions (5%). The pass mark is 60%.

- **Performance Certificate:** in a Performance Certificate you play five pieces. Up to three of these can be Free Choice Pieces. Each song is marked out of 20 and the pass mark is 60%.

## Book Contents

The book is divided into a number of sections:

- **Exam Pieces:** in this book you will find six specially commissioned pieces of Grade 4 standard. Each of these is preceded by a *Fact File*, and each single Fact File contains a summary of the song, its style, tempo, key and technical features, along with a list of the musicians who played on it. Also included is more in-depth information on the genre it is styled upon and relevant techniques you will encounter, as well as recommended further listening. The song itself is printed on two pages and immediately after each song is a *Walkthrough*. This covers the whole song from a performance perspective, focusing on the technical issues you will encounter along the way. Each Walkthrough features two graphical musical 'highlights' showing particular parts of the song. Each song comes with a full mix version and a backing track. Both versions have spoken count-ins at the beginning. Please note that any solos played on the full mix versions are indicative only.

- **Technical Exercises:** you should prepare the exercises set in this grade as indicated. There is also a Fill test that should be practised and played to the backing track.

- **Supporting Tests and General Musicianship Questions:** in Bass Grade 4 there are three supporting tests. You can choose *either* a Sight Reading test *or* an Improvisation & Interpretation test (please choose only one of those), which is then followed by the two mandatory Ear Tests and a set of General Musicianship Questions (GMQs). Examples of the types of tests likely to appear in the exam are printed in this book, while additional examples of both types of tests and the GMQs can be found in the Rockschool *Bass Companion Guide*.

- **Grade 5 Preview:** in this book we have included one of the songs featured in the Grade 5 Bass book as a taster. The piece is printed with its accompanying Fact File and Walkthrough, and the full mix and backing tracks are on the CD.

- **General Information:** finally, you will find the information you need on exam procedures, including online examination entry, marking schemes and what to do when arriving (and waiting) for your exam.

We hope you enjoy using this book. You will find a *Syllabus Guide* for Bass and other exam information on our website: *www.rockschool.co.uk*. Rockschool Graded Music Exams are accredited in England, Wales and Northern Ireland by Ofqual, the DfE and CCEA and by SQA Accreditation in Scotland.

SONG TITLE: 223
GENRE: POP PUNK
TEMPO: 165 BPM
KEY: D MAJOR

TECH FEATURES: RIFFING ON ONE STRING
FAST TEMPOS
DYNAMICS

COMPOSER: JAMES UINGS

PERSONNEL: STUART RYAN (GTR)
DAVE MARKS (BASS)
NOAM LEDERMAN (DRUMS)

## OVERVIEW

'223' is a fast-paced pop punk track written in the style of bands such as Blink-182, The Offspring, Sum 41 and Green Day. Pop punk basslines are often melodic, riff-based and tough to play due to the fast tempos used within the genre. This piece can be played either with the fingers or a pick, although for a true pop punk tone a pick is recommended.

## STYLE FOCUS

Pop punk is a combination of the fast tempos and chord progressions of punk fused with the catchy melodies of pop. The pop punk bassist will need the ability to play fast, melodic basslines that support the song and drive it forward. These basslines can often be memorable, and it is not uncommon for them to serve as counter melodies.

## THE BIGGER PICTURE

This blend of pop and punk styles has proved extremely durable over the last three decades. Early pop punk bands included Buzzcocks, Ramones and The Undertones, who were all discernible from their punk peers thanks to their strong melodies and less

political lyrical content. Pop punk became popular again during the mid-1990s thanks to bands such as Green Day and The Offspring, the latter of which found mainstream success through tracks like 'Come Out And Play'.

By the end of the 1990s pop punk had become a worldwide phenomenon and Blink-182, Less Than Jake and Sum 41, among others, enjoyed widespread popularity alongside existing pop punk groups like the aforementioned Green Day and The Offspring.

The focal point of pop punk is often the guitars or vocals, but bassists Mike Dirnt (Green Day), Greg K (The Offspring) and Mark Hoppus (Blink-182) attract more attention than bassists in some other genres, thanks to the melodic flavour of pop punk.

## RECOMMENDED LISTENING

Classic pop punk albums include Green Day's *Dookie* (1994), boasting their first big hit 'Longview', and *Warning* (2000), which includes the title track and 'Minority'. *Americana* by The Offspring (1998) is also recommended for Greg K's basslines on 'Pretty Fly (For a White Guy)'. *Enema of The State* (1999) by Blink-182 also offers a feel for pop punk basslines on 'What's My Age Again' and 'All The Small Things'.

EQ: FINGER PICK = TREBLE/HIGH ↑ +
MID = ↓ −
BASS = 0 → +↑

**James Uings**

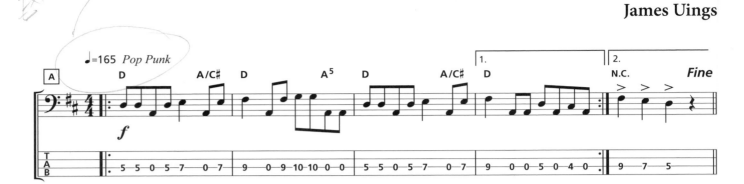

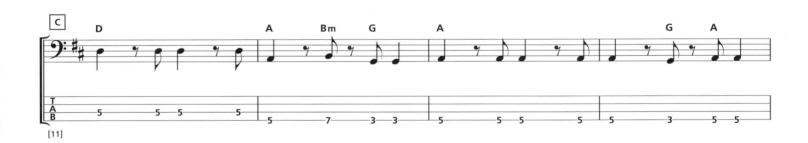

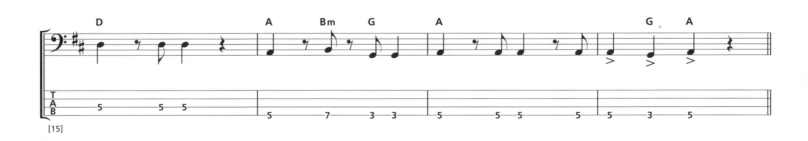

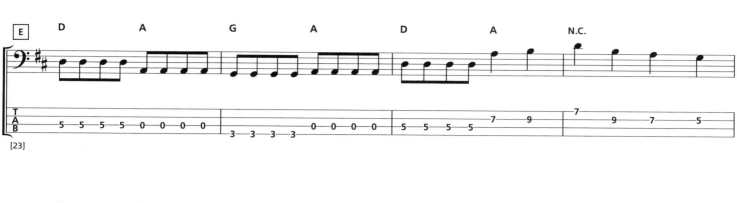

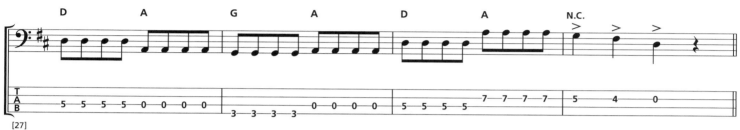

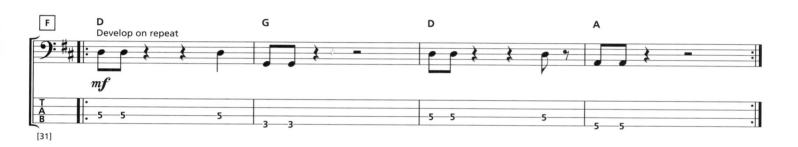

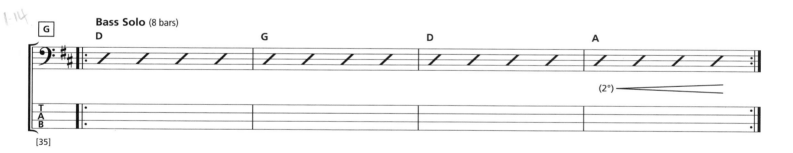

# Walkthrough

## A Section (Bars 1–6)
The intro to '223' has a melodic bassline that outlines the chord progression and is played entirely on one string.

**Bars 1–6** | *Bass riff*
The bass riff that opens '223' is a melodic line based on chord tones, alternating with the open A string. Fret the D with your first finger then move up to fret the E at the end of the first bar with the same finger. Use your first and second fingers to play the F# and G notes.

**Bars 1–6** | *Timing*
The bass is the featured instrument and for the first four bars the drums and guitar play minimal parts only. Focus on your timing because it will be noticeable if you slow down or speed up in between the drum and guitar hits.

## B Section (Bars 6–10)
The B section is based on an eighth-note line that focuses on the root notes of the guitar chords.

**Bars 6–8** | *Consistent eighth notes*
This is a continuous eighth-note line that must be played with a consistent attack throughout. If you are using a pick, play this part using up and downstrokes and ensure you produce the same level of attack and volume with each.

## C Section (Bars 11–18)
A different feel is used for the verse. This is a classic pop punk progression and features some quick positional shifts.

**Bar 14** | *Syncopation*
In this bar, there are some notes played on offbeats (Fig. 1). These occur on the offbeats of beats two and three. It can be tricky to count this rhythm at the song's fast tempo, so play this part slowly to begin with. Notes should fall on beat one, on the offbeats of beats two and three, then on beat four. Concentrate on locking in with the guitar.

## D Section (Bars 19–22)
The bassline here has the same rhythmic pattern in the first three bars and locks in tightly with the drum part.

**Bars 19–22** | *Rhythm*
The rhythm in this section is simpler than it looks. The first two notes are both eighth notes that fall on the first and second beats. These are followed by a group of four eighth notes played on the third and fourth beats.

**Bars 19–22** | *Melodic lines*
Each chord is connected in the bassline by the group of four

eighth notes in each bar (Fig. 2). These groups are melodic lines that use diatonic notes to link the chords together.

## E and F Sections (Bars 23–34)
The E section is essentially a repeat of the line from the B section. The F section has a light reggae feel with a simple yet effective bass part.

## G Section (Bars 35–38)
The bass solo section is an opportunity to improvise a solo that fits the style of the song.

**Bars 35–38** | *Soloing*
When planning your bass solo, consider the notes in each chord. Write these down then try to find melodic phrases that use these notes. You could take inspiration from the melodic linking phrases that were used in the bridge section.

## H Section (Bars 39–45)
This is a repeat of the D section with some variations. There are also some navigation markings to be aware of.

**Bar 45** | *Navigation*
At the end of the extended bridge section you are directed back to the beginning of the song, where the intro is played again as an outro. Be sure to stop at the direction 'Fine' at the end of the second time bar.

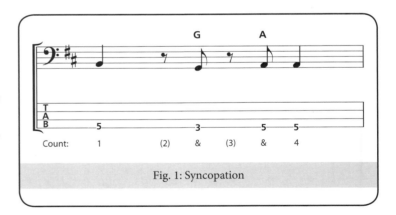
Fig. 1: Syncopation

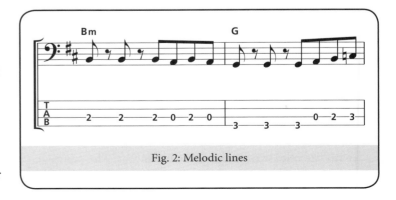
Fig. 2: Melodic lines

SONG TITLE:  BOOTSYLICIOUS
GENRE:  FUNK
TEMPO:  105 BPM
KEY:  F MAJOR

TECH FEATURES:  DOUBLE-STOPS
VIBRATO

COMPOSER:  LUKE ALDRIDGE

PERSONNEL:  STUART RYAN (GTR)
HENRY THOMAS (BASS)
NOAM LEDERMAN (DRUMS)
ROSS STANLEY (KEYS)
FERGUS GERRAND (PERC)
FULL FAT HORNS (BRASS)

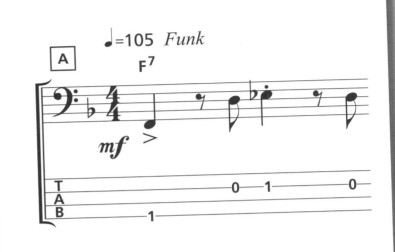

## OVERVIEW

'Bootsylicious' is a funk track that brings to mind the legendary, influential and flamboyant funk bassist Bootsy Collins. The bassline on 'Bootsylicious' is a classic funk line that has been created using doublestops and ornamental features such as shakes. As with all funk music, there is a lot of scope within this piece for improvisation once you feel comfortable playing the notated parts.

## STYLE FOCUS

Funk is fun for bass players to play and will expand your vocabulary. The bass guitar is regularly the focal point of this style and is called upon to play slapped lines, syncopated fingerstyle grooves and chordal parts. It is also common for bassists to use effects such as envelope filters, octave dividers and fuzz pedals when playing funk music. Despite the freedom often given to the bass player in funk, it is important to remember that the groove is always the main priority.

## THE BIGGER PICTURE

James Brown arguably created funk in 1967 with the release of his single 'Cold Sweat'. The song featured a strong emphasis on the first beat of each bar ('the one') and a drum groove that has become synonymous with the genre.

Bootsy Collins joined James Brown's band in 1970 after Brown fired his existing group following an argument over wages. Collins was with Brown for less than a year yet he played on some of his most iconic recordings, including 'Get Up (I Feel Like Being A) Sex Machine' and 'Super Bad'. Bootsy was 18 years old.

After leaving Brown, Collins joined George Clinton's P-Funk, where he developed the effects-heavy style that became his signature. In 1978, he released his third solo album titled *Bootsy? Player Of The Year* that contained the hit song 'Bootzilla'.

## RECOMMENDED LISTENING

Classic Bootsy Collins tracks include James Brown's 'Sex Machine', which features an improvised funk bassline that develops continuously throughout the song. With Parliament, Collins is at his best on 'P-Funk (Wants To Get Funked Up)' and 'Mothership Connection (Star Child)', both from the classic *Mothership Connection* (1975) album. 'Hollwood Squares' and 'Bootzilla' from his solo album *Bootsy? Player Of The Year* are not to be missed.

# Bootsylicious

**Luke Aldridge**

[25]

[29]

**Trombone Solo** (7 bars)
Improvise bass line

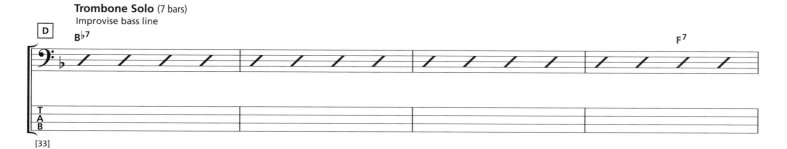

[33]

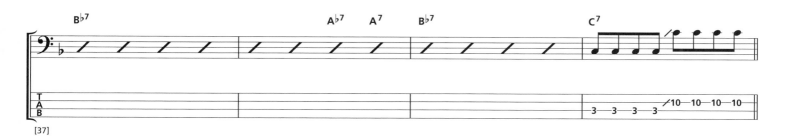

[37]

[41]

[45]

Bass Grade 4

# Walkthrough

## A Section (Bars 1–16)
The opening section establishes a classic funk bass groove that relies heavily on timing and use of dynamics.

### Bars 1–2 | *Funk groove*
This classic funk groove uses the root note (F), the 6th (D) and the 7th (E♭) as its basis (Fig. 1). This grouping of notes can be heard in countless funk grooves throughout the genre. When playing this part, take note of the articulation markings: the first note is accented and it is important that you follow this. It is all about a strong downbeat at the beginning of the bar. Many of the other notes in this part are marked staccato, so be sure to play them as such to produce the correct feel.

### Bar 2 | *Vibrato*
You should add vibrato to the final note in bar 2 and you can do this by moving the note up and down a small amount with your finger, or by using a side to side movement. Whichever method you adopt, make sure that the movement is consistent in both timing and pitch otherwise you will sound out of tune.

### Bar 8 | *Triplet fill*
There is a triplet fill on the third beat of this bar. Remember that triplets should consist of three evenly played notes. Practise the triplet using the vocalisation 'ev-en-ly' in order to ensure you are playing it as a triplet.

## B Section (Bars 17–24)
The next section of the piece moves to a B♭7 chord and features a different bassline that is based heavily on the dominant 7th arpeggio.

### Bars 17–18 | *Chord tones*
The bassline for this section is constructed from chord tones of the B♭7 chord: B♭ (root), F (5th) and A♭ (♭7th).

## C Section (Bars 25–32)
The harmony returns to F7 in this section and the original groove is re-introduced. However, there are some new parts that are heavily syncopated.

### Bars 26–31 | *Syncopation*
You will encounter some tricky syncopations here. The notes on the third beat are played on the second and fourth 16th notes of the beat. You may find the first note easier to place if you practise by playing a quiet ghost note with your picking hand on the third beat, then play the note (E♭) immediately afterwards. You can remove this when you feel comfortable with the timing. The next note should fall just before the downbeat of beat four. The final note of the bar occurs in the same place (i.e. directly before the downbeat of the next bar).

### Bar 28 | *Accents*
There are two groups of four 16th notes to play in this bar. Note that the last note of each grouping is marked with both a staccato dot and an accent (Fig. 2) and be sure to place a heavy accent on this note as well as playing it as short as you can, as indicated.

## D Section (Bars 33–40)
This section has no written bass part and therefore provides you the opportunity to improvise a bassline.

### Bars 33–40 | *Improvising a bassline*
You should create your own bassline here. You are free to play as you wish but should create a part that is in keeping with the style of the rest of the piece.

## E Section (Bars 41–48)
The closing part of 'Bootsylicious' reintroduces the original bassline and features some embellishments before the final two bar concluding line.

### Bar 47 | *Pull-offs*
To execute a clean pull-off you should pull your finger off the string using a snapping movement towards to the floor. Don't pull too hard or too slowly or you risk bending the string out of tune.

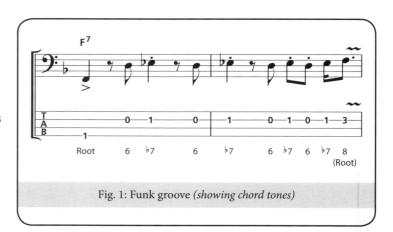

Fig. 1: Funk groove *(showing chord tones)*

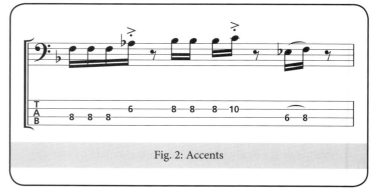

Fig. 2: Accents

SONG TITLE:    HYDE IN THE PARK
GENRE:         CLASSIC ROCK
TEMPO:         126 BPM
KEY:           G MAJOR

TECH FEATURES:  OCTAVE FIGURES
                PENTATONIC LINES
                MELODIC PLAYING

COMPOSER:       JOE BENNETT

PERSONNEL:      STUART RYAN (GTR)
                HENRY THOMAS (BASS)
                NOAM LEDERMAN (DRUMS)
                FERGUS GERRAND (PERC)

## OVERVIEW

'Hyde In The Park' is a classic rock track in the style of bands like the Rolling Stones, The Small Faces, The Yardbirds and The Who. The bassline for this song is an inventive and highly melodic line that features octave riffs, arpeggio figures and pentatonic lines; all common features from this era of rock bass playing.

## STYLE FOCUS

Improvisation is an important element of classic rock and one that points to the influence of blues on the genre. This is most evident in its lead guitar solos. However, since the 1960s classic rock bassists have been keen to explore their instrument too and many rock songs of that decade feature melodic basslines that were often improvisational in nature.

## THE BIGGER PICTURE

Rock music developed in the mid 1960s when musicians strove to combine the sounds of rock 'n' roll, blues, country and, to a lesser extent, folk and jazz. The guitar quickly became the focal point of most acts and a basic instrumentation of guitars, bass, drums and vocals (sometimes augmented by piano) was common. Although the styles that flowed into classic rock were mainly American, British groups were instrumental in the creation of the genre. The first wave was known as the British Invasion; a term used to describe the number of British groups who became popular in America during the 1960s. The Beatles and the Rolling Stones led the pack, with The Kinks (who were later banned from playing in the country) and The Dave Clark Five following hot on their heels. In the 1970s Led Zeppelin continued to dominate the genre.

There were many noteworthy bass players in this genre during the 1960s (and onwards), including Paul McCartney (The Beatles), Bill Wyman (Rolling Stones), John Entwistle (The Who), Jack Bruce (Cream) and Andy Fraser (Free).

## RECOMMENDED LISTENING

The Rolling Stones recorded many classic rock singles, including '(I Can't Get No) Satisfaction', 'Brown Sugar' and 'Honky Tonk Woman'. All can be found on their compilation *Hot Rocks 1964–1971*. Other examples include 'Wham Bam, Thank You Mam' by The Small Faces, 'Hush' by Deep Purple, and 'My Generation' by The Who. The Yardbirds' 'Shapes Of Things' is also recommended.

# Hyde In The Park

Joe Bennett

# Walkthrough

## A Section (Bars 1–4)
The intro to this song is a four bar section comprising of an octave-based line on the bass.

### Bars 1–3 | *Octaves*
The bass plays an eighth-note octave line here. The string crossing is a little awkward, so practise this part slowly and alternate the fingers on your picking hand where possible.

## B Section (Bars 5–12)
This section of the piece is based around a two bar riff on a G major chord and makes use of the major pentatonic scale.

### Bar 6 | *Staccato notes*
The three staccato quarter notes played here act as a response to the first bar of the sequence (Fig. 1). Play these notes short and detached by releasing pressure on the string.

## C Section (Bars 13–20)
The bassline now moves between D and C chords and, once again, makes use of the pentatonic scale.

### Bar 13–16 | *Pentatonics*
In bars 13 and 15, you will see the D and C major pentatonic scales used over the D and C chords. These scales are applied in the same pattern as in the verse. Slide into the F♯ in bar 13 with your fourth finger, leaving the other fingers free to play the rest of the notes. The same is true in bar 15.

### Bar 20 | *Non-diatonic chords*
In bar 20 there are two chords that do not belong to the key of G major: E♭ and F. These chords are non-diatonic and have been 'borrowed' from the parallel minor key to create an interesting approach back to G (via the F) for the D section. This chord progression is common in rock music.

## D Section (Bars 21–36)
The bassline for this section is a busy melodic line that features extensive use of arpeggios.

### Bars 21–22 | *Use of arpeggios*
The D section uses a basic chord progression of G, F and C, and the bass part clearly outlines these chords using arpeggios (Fig. 2). The first note of each arpeggio is played on the upbeat of the previous beat, in effect anticipating the chord (sometimes referred to as a 'push').

### Bar 32 | *Bass fill*
Start slowly and gradually build up speed as you become more confident with the phrase. After outlining the F major arpeggio (with the root tied from the previous bar), the

bassline slides up to the C at the 10th fret of the D string to outline the C major chord. This is followed by an E, which is the major 3rd. This E is embellished by briefly moving up to the F a semitone above and then back down.

## E & F Sections (Bars 37–52)
The bass plays a lot of melodic fills during this section, and is the featured instrument in the arrangement.

### Bars 37–38 | *Melodic fills*
The first fill played here is anticipated at the end of bar 37. The B (preceded by a quick B♭ grace note) is tied across the bar and followed by a series of eighth notes from the major pentatonic scale. Using the third finger of your fretting hand on the B will allow you to play all of the other notes using the one-finger-per-fret system.

### Bars 43–48 | *Developing a part*
After playing several similar fills in bars 37–42, you have the opportunity here to develop this part yourself. When you develop a part you should make sure you are faithful to the original that is notated while still taking the section somewhere new. Common ways to develop a part are to vary the rhythm and note choices. These are, of course, only suggestions and you should play the part which you feel works best. Remember the part should be in keeping with the style of the piece.

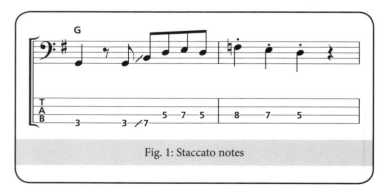

Fig. 1: Staccato notes

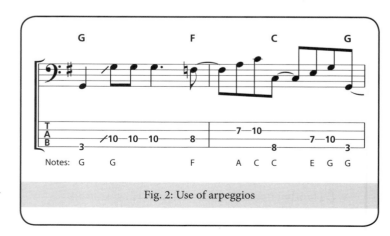

Fig. 2: Use of arpeggios

SONG TITLE: B & B SCENE
GENRE: BLUES
TEMPO: 140 BPM
KEY: Bb BLUES

TECH FEATURES: EIGHTH-NOTE LINES
IMPROVISATION
CONSISTENCY

COMPOSER: ALISON RAYNER

PERSONNEL: STUART RYAN (GTR)
HENRY THOMAS (BASS)
NOAM LEDERMAN (DRUMS)
ROSS STANLEY (KEYS)
FERGUS GERRAND (PERC)
FULL FAT HORNS (BRASS)

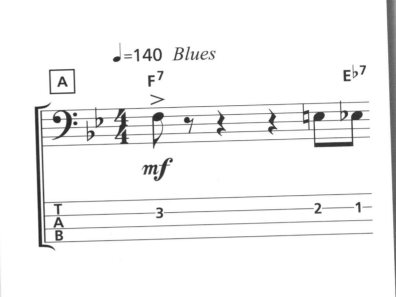

## OVERVIEW

'B & B Scene' is an uptempo blues track in the style of B.B. King, Muddy Waters and T-Bone Walker. It is an example of a 12-bar blues and features eighth-note lines and improvisation among its techniques.

## STYLE FOCUS

This piece follows the traditional 12-bar blues formula. The bassline, which is based on chord and scale tones, derives from the walking basslines heard on many jazz songs. This line features a basic melodic idea that is then transposed over the different chords. This can be embellished further by incorporating chromatic lines to the chord changes.

## THE BIGGER PICTURE

The blues began in the black communities of America's southern states. It has its roots in the music of the slaves who were captured and sailed from their homelands to the New World, where their own musical traditions mingled with European folk styles and church music. The first mention of blues on record occurred in 1903 when Memphis band leader W C Handy encountered a man at a train station in rural Mississippi who sang "the weirdest music", backing himself with slide guitar. In the late 1920s Blind Lemon Jefferson made a series of recordings of songs that defined the blues genre. Charley Patton, Robert Johnson and Son House soon followed suit, performing their own acoustic blues.

After the Second World War, the blues went electric as guitarists like B.B. King, Muddy Waters and T-Bone Walker mastered the new technology that was the electric guitar. The style has remained popular since the British Blues Boom of the 1960s when English guitarists like Eric Clapton and Peter Green mastered the licks of their heroes and turned up the distortion.

Blues bassists such as Tommy Shannon (Stevie Ray Vaughan), Roscoe Beck (Robben Ford) and Nathan East (Eric Clapton) will inspire you.

## RECOMMENDED LISTENING

Blues compilations are a good place to start. *Blues Masters: The Very Best of T-Bone Walker* and *B.B. King: The Complete Collection* with 'Every Day I Have The Blues' and 'The Thrill Is Gone'. Track down *Muddy Waters: The Anthology 1947–1972* for 'Hoochie Coochie Man'. John Mayall's *Blues Breakers With Eric Clapton* is a British Blues Boom classic.

# B & B Scene

**Alison Rayner**

# Walkthrough

## A Section (Bars 1–4)
The intro to this song features a simple riff based on the blues scale and played in unison with the guitar.

**Bars 1–3 | *Unison riff***
After an initial F on the first beat, the unison riff starts on the fourth beat of the bar. This line moves chromatically down from the F to the E♭ via an E natural. The E is the blue note of the B♭ blues scale, employed for the majority of this line. The only note in this line that does not belong to the scale is the G at the end of the second bar.

## B Section (Bars 5–16)
The main bass groove is introduced during this section with walking bass figures to connect the chords.

**Bars 5–7 | *Main bass groove***
The main part of the line appears here. The line itself is a one bar figure (Fig. 1) used over each of the three chords. Eighth notes and several chord tones appear: the root (B♭), the octave (B♭), the 7th (A♭), and the 5th (F). The G at the beginning of the fourth beat is used as a passing note.

**Bars 5–7 | *Consistency***
The main groove is melodic and plays a supportive role. Ensure that you play the eighth notes evenly.

**Bar 8 | *Connecting lines***
This ascending line creates a smooth transition to the E♭7 chord. After the root note is played on beat one, the second degree of the scale is played (in this case a C) then the part moves up chromatically on the two remaining beats.

## C Section (Bars 17–28)
This is a unison line played with the guitar and organ.

**Bars 17–18 | *Call and response***
This line is a call and response part. The phrase in bar 17 is 'answered' by the phrase in bar 18. Be sure to lock in with the other instruments during this section and note how this line should be played a lot quieter than the previous part.

## D Section (Bars 29–40)
During the guitar solo, a new bassline is introduced. This line is also a repeating one bar motif and uses the same connecting lines to link the chords.

**Bar 29 | *Bass groove***
This line consists of eighth notes on the first three beats, and a quarter note on the fourth beat. It is a descending line which moves from the root (B♭), to the 7th (A♭), to the 5th (F)

via a passing note (G). The G is played again on the fourth beat. Although the G is not part of the chord, this scale tone is commonly used in blues basslines.

## E Section (Bars 41–52)
The guitar and organ play the phrases heard during the verse section and the bass responds with an improvised fill. The final seven bars are an opportunity for you to solo freely.

**Bars 41–44 | *Improvised fills***
When improvising the fills, ensure that your phrases are short statements that do not last beyond one bar each. The blues scale is the most obvious scale selection.

## F Section (Bars 53–69)
This final section introduces a slightly different bassline and finishes with an adapted repeat of the A section.

**Bar 53 | *Variation on the bassline***
In this variation on the established line, the 3rd and the 5th of the chord are played as eighth notes on the second beat. If you start this bar with the second finger of your fretting hand on the B♭, you will find it is then simple to play the D with your first finger, and the F with your fourth (Fig. 2).

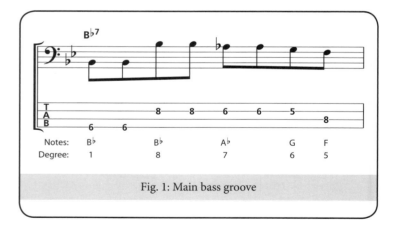

Fig. 1: Main bass groove

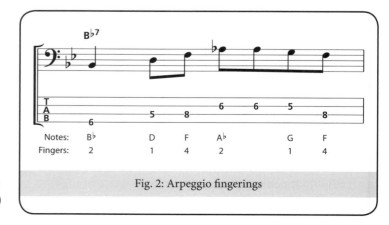

Fig. 2: Arpeggio fingerings

SONG TITLE: NOISY NEIGHBOUR

GENRE: INDIE ROCK

TEMPO: 135 BPM

KEY: C# MINOR

TECH FEATURES: FAST FILLS
PULL-OFFS
GHOST NOTES

COMPOSER: NOAM LEDERMAN

PERSONNEL: STUART RYAN (GTR)
DAVE MARKS (BASS)
NOAM LEDERMAN (DRUMS)

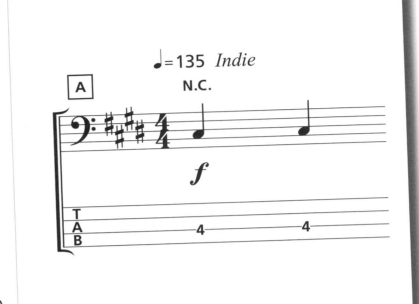

## OVERVIEW

'Noisy Neighbour' is an indie rock track in the style of Arctic Monkeys, Franz Ferdinand and The Kooks. The bassline on this indie flavoured song is heavily riff based and features some unusual twists and turns that will capture your attention and entertain. Indie rock can be played with either the fingers or a pick, although most indie rock bassists favour a pick.

## STYLE FOCUS

This particular form of indie rock is fast-paced and great fun for bass players. Many of the parts are riff-based and integral to the song. While indie rock places the focus on lyrical content and attitude rather than musical proficiency, it is nevertheless vital that the bass and drums lock tightly together. A solid foundation is as important in this style of music as it is in any other.

## THE BIGGER PICTURE

Indie rock (short for 'independent') is a term that was originally used to describe rock music that was recorded on a low budget and self-released, promoted and financed rather than 'bought' and distributed by a major record label. The style is home to a range of sub-genres, unified (mostly) in an enduring spirit of independence and artistic credibility.

Freedom from major labels has allowed indie rockers to exercise complete creative control over their music and, as such, create interesting sounds and style motifs. The DIY approach of indie's early days lives on in the opportunities for self-promotion presented by MySpace and Facebook, and the ability to raise funds via Pledge Music.

This form of indie rock shows some similarities to pop punk but often with a rougher edge to its production. The basic instrumentation of guitars, bass, drums and vocals is common, as are fast tempos and punk-inspired simple chord progressions.

## RECOMMENDED LISTENING

The debut album by Arctic Monkeys, *Whatever People Say I Am, That's What I'm Not* (2006) was the fastest-selling debut album in British chart history thanks to the singles 'I Bet You Look Good On The Dancefloor', and 'When The Sun Goes Down'. Franz Ferdinand's self-titled debut album (2004), released by Domino, is also a great starting point, particularly the tracks 'The Dark Of The Matinee' and 'Take Me Out'.

# Noisy Neighbour

**Noam Lederman**

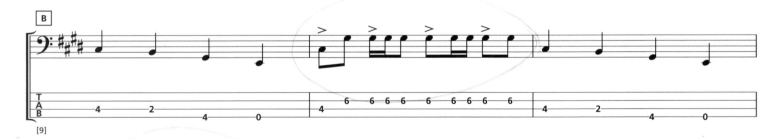

# Walkthrough

## A Section (Bars 1–8)
The intro introduces a unison riff based around the tritone interval, which is a key feature of this piece.

**Bar 1 | *Riff***
The main riff is introduced after the opening drum fill. Two quarter note C♯'s are played, followed by the 5th, a G♯, which then drops down to a G, the flattened 5th. This interval (C♯–G, in this case) is known as the tritone. It is normally used to give a sinister quality (as on the title track of *Black Sabbath*, the debut album from the band of the same name).

**Bar 1 | *Rhythmic accuracy***
The G♯–G figure is played with a tricky rhythm. The G♯ is played on beat three, with the G natural occurring on the last 16th note of the same beat. It is effectively played just before the fourth beat, anticipating it. The note is then tied into the fourth beat and the next note is played on the '&' of beat four.

**Bar 6 | *Root and fifth variation***
Two additional notes are added to the second beat here: a G♯ and a C♯, played on the D and G strings, respectively. Combined with the C♯ on beat one, these make a root-5th-octave figure common to most styles of music.

## B Section (Bars 9–17)
A bar of quarter notes comprise this new unison riff. This powerful line is then followed by some bass fills.

**Bar 10 | *Sixteenth-note fill***
After playing the root note, the bass slides up to the 5th (G♯) and plays an eighth note and 16th-note rhythm. Be careful of the accented notes here.

**Bar 12 | *Pull-off fill***
This bass fill is more complex than the one in bar 11 (Fig. 1). A descending fill starts on the second beat from the C♯ an octave above the root. This line uses the natural minor scale. Beware of the accented notes and add the pull-offs where written to smooth out the line.

## C Section (Bars 18–30)
This section features a new groove based around chord tones, while the idea established in the first bar is reused over the different chords. You also have the opportunity to develop your own variations of the basic groove.

**Bars 18–21 | *Bass groove***
This line begins on the root of the chord (E), followed by the E an octave higher. An A is then played as an approach note to B, the 5th of the chord. Essentially, this line is based

around the root, 5th and octave, with the A used as an approach note. The following bars use a similar sequence of notes as the chords change, and the part is developed in the following four bars.

## D Section (Bars 31–34)
This repeat of the verse section provides an opportunity for you to improvise your own bass fills.

**Bars 31–34 | *Improvised bass fills***
The bass fills in this section follow the quarter-note riff played with the guitar. You only have three beats available for each fill, and you must be careful not to overrun. Base your ideas on the fills used in the first verse section. The minor pentatonic scale and blues scale will both be suitable choices for fills here.

## E Section (Bars 35–44)
This section of the song is a continuous eighth-note groove with some ghost notes added for variety.

**Bar 36 | *Ghost notes***
Many of the notes in this bar are played as ghost notes (Fig. 2). Ghost notes are pitchless notes that are played by lifting the fretting hand fingers slightly off the string to mute them. Make sure that you accent the pitched notes as indicated here.

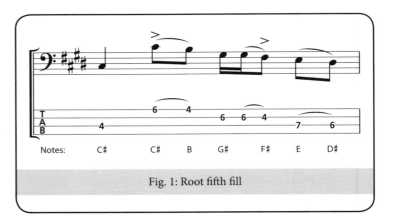

Fig. 1: Root fifth fill

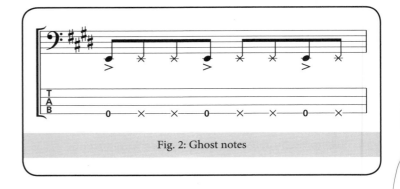

Fig. 2: Ghost notes

SONG TITLE: BENSON BURNER
GENRE: JAZZ
TEMPO: 104 BPM
KEY: A MINOR

TECH FEATURES: MELODIC LINES
IMPROVISATION
SYNCOPATION

COMPOSER: DEIRDRE CARTWRIGHT

PERSONNEL: STUART RYAN (GTR)
HENRY THOMAS (BASS)
NOAM LEDERMAN (DRUMS)
ROSS STANLEY (KEYS)
FERGUS GERRAND (PERC)

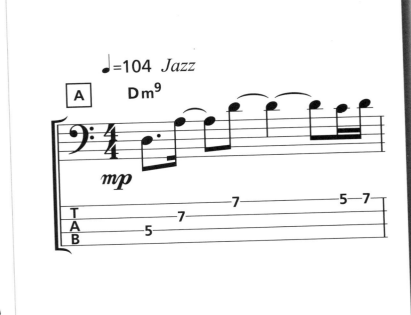

## OVERVIEW

'Benson Burner' tips its hat to smooth jazz artists such as George Benson, Chet Atkins, Lee Ritenour and David Sanborn. The bassline for this piece is typical of the genre and while supportive, it is also melodic and offers plenty of scope for improvisation. It is common for the bass player to take a solo in this style. This piece provides that opportunity.

## STYLE FOCUS

Improvisation is a huge element of all styles of jazz and it plays a prominent part here, both in the lead guitar parts and the bassline. The electric bass is more common than the traditional upright bass in this style of smooth jazz, and many bass players have made a name for themselves playing this particular style.

## THE BIGGER PICTURE

Jazz, much like rock, is an umbrella term that covers a broad range of sub-genres. This particular sub-genre is often referred to as smooth jazz because of its radio friendly combination of funk, R&B and jazz. The more traditional elements of jazz, however, are not included; for example, the swing feel and

walking basslines). Smooth jazz is often instrumental, with a featured soloist playing melody lines then soloing over the accompaniment.

The genre was popularised by guitarist Wes Montgomery in the late 1960s when he began recording instrumental covers of pop tunes by The Beatles and other bands. His producer, Creed Taylor, used the popularity of these albums to found a record label called CTI Records that specialised in smooth jazz. During the 1970s, many jazz musicians released smooth jazz records on the label, including David Sanborn, George Benson and Lee Ritenour.

Smooth jazz has produced many excellent bassists including Marcus Miller, Scott Ambrose (Spyro Gyra) and Nathan East (Fourplay).

## RECOMMENDED LISTENING

'Morning Dance' by Spyro Gyra was a top 40 hit in America in 1979, and 'This Masquerade', 'Breezin'' and 'Give Me The Night' by George Benson, found on *The George Benson Collection* (1988), had a similar level of success. Lee Ritenour's 'Rio' and 'Run For Cover' are superb examples of smooth jazz in action, and a great opportunity to hear the legendary bassist Marcus Miller in action.

# Benson Burner

### Deirdre Cartwright

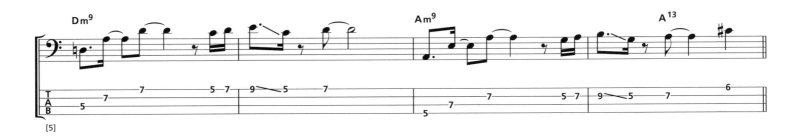

# Walkthrough

## A Section (Bars 1–8)
The first section of this piece features a melodic bassline that clearly outlines the chord progression.

### Bars 1–2 | *Rhythms*
The main bass figure is played with a syncopated rhythm. The root note D is played on beat one and the A is played on the final 16th note of the beat. This note is then tied into the second beat and the octave D is played on the upbeat. This note should be held until the second half of the fourth beat where two 16th notes are played.

### Bars 1–2 | *Melodic bassline*
The main figure is based around a root-fifth-octave motif. This is embellished in the second bar where the bass moves up to the E, which is the 9th in the Dm$^9$ chord. This note then slides down to the 7th of the chord (C) then returns to the D (Fig. 1). This is a great example of chord tones being used to create a melodic phrase. This idea is repeated over the Am$^9$ chord in the following two bars.

## B Section (Bars 9–16)
This section has more chordal movement and requires a different bass part. There is a walking bassline, a common device in jazz based music.

### Bars 9–12 | *Walking bassline*
A walking bassline is used here. The chords change every two beats, so the bassline uses chord tones and chromatic passing notes to outline the harmony. In bar 11 the bass plays the root (F) and 3rd (A) of the F$^7$ chord, followed by the 3rd (G♯) and root of the E$^{7♯9}$ chord (Fig. 2).

### Bars 15–16 | *Syncopation*
These two bars feature a heavily syncopated rhythm. In bar 15, the first two F notes are played as straight eighth notes, although the first should be played staccato. The next F is played on the second 16th note of the second beat. You may find it easier to think of this note as occurring just after the second beat, rather than trying to count it. The fourth F is played on beat three.

## C Section (Bars 17–24)
This section is a repeat of the bassline from the A section, except it contains some small embellishments.

### Bar 18 | *Melodic embellishments*
A small embellishment is added to the line in this bar. After playing the 9th-7th-root figure described earlier, a hammer-on/pull-off figure is played between the 7th and the root (C and D). The C is played on the final 16th note of beat three, followed by a D and a C played as eighth notes on beat four.

This phrase is played as a hammer-on/pull-off, so only play the string once with your picking hand.

## D Section (Bars 25–44)
There is a sparse bassline throughout the first four bars of this section, then the line from the A section is reintroduced with some small variations.

### Bar 27 | *Syncopation*
The two-note figure from the previous bars is used again here and followed by a syncopated line that starts on the second beat. This three note figure starts on the second 16th note of the beat, so avoid playing this line too early. The following bar reuses the syncopated rhythm previously used at the end of the B section.

## E Section (Bars 45–52)
The song ends with a six bar improvised bass solo capped with the two bar figure as used as part of the D section.

### Bars 45–50 | *Bass solo*
You are required to improvise a solo over this section. Before doing so, you may like to write down the notes from each of the chords so you can focus on these notes during your solo.

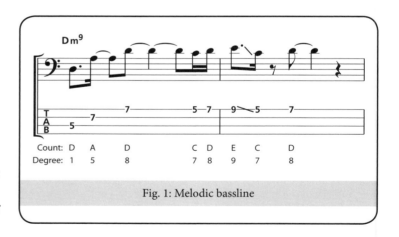

Fig. 1: Melodic bassline

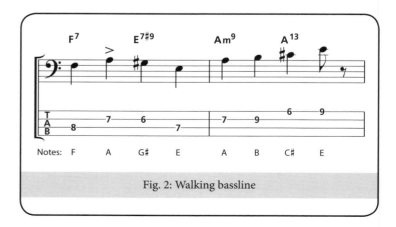

Fig. 2: Walking bassline

# Technical Exercises

In this section the examiner will ask you to play a selection of exercises drawn from each of the three groups shown below. Groups A and B contain examples of the scales and arpeggios you can use when playing the pieces. In Group C you will be asked to prepare the bassline riff exercise and play it to the backing track in the exam. You do not need to memorise the exercises (and can use the book in the exam) but the examiner will be looking for the speed of your response. The examiner will also give credit for the level of your musicality.

Groups A and B should be prepared on the starting notes indicated. Before you start the section you will be asked whether you would like to play the exercises along with the click or hear a single bar of click before you commence the test. The tempo is ♩ = 80.

**Group A: Scales**
One octave prepared from the starting notes A, B, C and D

1. Natural minor scale (A natural minor scale shown)

2. Minor pentatonic scale (B minor pentatonic scale shown)

3. Blues scale (C blues scale shown)

One octave from the starting notes F and B♭

1. Major scale (F major scale shown)

2. Major pentatonic scale (B♭ major pentatonic scale shown)

### Group B: Arpeggios

One octave prepared from the starting notes A, B, C and D

1. Major arpeggio (B major arpeggio shown)

2. Minor arpeggio (C minor arpeggio shown)

3. Dominant 7 arpeggio (D dominant 7 arpeggio shown)

## Group C: Riff

In the exam you will be asked to play the following riff to a backing track. The riff shown in bars 1 and 2 should be played in the same shape in bars 3–8. The root note of the pattern to be played is shown in the music in bars 3, 5 and 7. The tempo is ♩= 100.

# Sight Reading

In this section you have a choice between either a sight reading test or an improvisation and interpretation test (see facing page). At this level there is an element of improvisation. This is in the form of a two bar development of the bassline. The piece will be composed in the style of rock, funk or blues and will have chord symbols throughout. The test is eight bars long and is in one of the following keys: D major or G major, or D minor or A minor. The examiner will allow you 90 seconds to prepare it and will set the tempo for you. The tempo is ♩ = 80–90.

# Improvisation & Interpretation

In Grade 4, the improvisation and interpretation tests contain a small amount of sight reading. This consists of a two bar section of groove notation at the beginning of each test. You will be asked to play the notated bassline and complete the test using an improvised line as indicated. This is played to a backing track of no more than eight bars. The test will be given in one of the four following keys: D major or G major, or D minor or A minor. You have 30 seconds to prepare then you will be allowed to practise during the first playing of the backing track before playing it to the examiner on the second playing of the backing track. This test is continuous with a one bar count-in at the beginning and after the practice session. The tempo is ♩=90–100.

# Ear Tests

There are two ear tests in this grade. The examiner will play each test to you twice. You will find one example of each type of test printed below.

### Test 1: Melodic Recall

The examiner will play you a two bar melody with a drum backing using either the D major pentatonic or B minor pentatonic scales. The first note of the melody will be the root note and the first interval will be descending. You will play the melody back on your instrument. You will hear the test twice.

Each time the test is played the sequence is: count-in, root note, count-in, melody. There will be a short gap for you to practise after you have heard the test for the second time. You will hear the count-in and root note for the third time followed by a vocal count-in and you will then play the melody to the drum backing. The tempo is ♩=90.

### Test 2: Harmonic Recall

The examiner will play you a tonic chord followed by a two bar chord sequence in the key of C major played to a guitar and drum backing. The sequence will be drawn from the I, IV and V chords and may occur in any combination. You will be asked to play the root notes of the chord sequence to the guitar and drum backing in the rhythm shown in the example below. You will then be asked to identify the chords. This rhythm will be used in all examples of this test given in the exam. You will hear the test twice.

Each time the test is played the sequence is: count-in, tonic, count-in, chords. There will be a short gap for you to practise after you have heard the test for the second time. You will hear the count-in and tonic for the third time followed by a vocal count-in and you will then play the root notes of the chords to the drum backing. You should then name the chord sequence. The tempo is ♩=90.

# General Musicianship Questions

In this part of the exam you will be asked five questions. Four of these questions will be about general music knowledge and the fifth question will be asked about your instrument.

## Music Knowledge

The examiner will ask you four music knowledge questions based on a piece of music that you have played in the exam. You will nominate the piece of music about which the questions will be asked. The scale question at the end of the list of subjects is mandatory.

*In Grade 4 you will be asked:*

- The names of pitches

- The meaning of the time signature and the key signature markings

- Repeat marks, first and second time bars, D.C., D.S., al Coda and al Fine markings

- Whole, half, quarter, eighth note, triplet eighth notes and 16$^{th}$ note values

- Whole, half, quarter, eighth note and 16$^{th}$ note rests and rest combinations

- The construction of major, minor or dominant$^7$ chords

- One type of scale that can be used appropriately in the solo section of the piece you have played

## Instrument Knowledge

The examiner will also ask you one question regarding your instrument.

*In Grade 4 you will be asked to identify/explain:*

- Any part or control on your bass

- The function of the volume and tone controls on your guitar

- The tone settings for the piece you have played on the amp and why you have chosen these settings

## Further Information

Tips on how to approach this part of this exam can be found in the *Syllabus Guide* for bass, the Rockschool *Bass Companion Guide* and on the Rockschool website: *www.rockschool.co.uk.*

# Entering Rockschool Exams

Entering a Rockschool exam is easy. You may enter either online at *www.rockschool.co.uk* or by downloading and filling in an exam entry form. Information on current exam fees can be obtained from Rockschool online or by calling +44 (0)845 460 4747.

- You should enter for your exam when you feel ready.

- You may enter for any one of the three examination periods shown below with their closing dates:

**EXAMINATION PERIODS**

| PERIOD | DURATION | CLOSING DATE |
|--------|----------|--------------|
| Period A | 1st February to 31st March | 1st December |
| Period B | 1st May to 31st July | 1st April |
| Period C | 23rd October to 15th December | 1st October |

*These dates apply from 1st September 2012 until further notice*

- The full Rockschool examination terms and conditions can be downloaded from our website. The information shown below is a summary.

- Please complete your entry with the information required. Fill in the type and level of exam and instrument, along with the examination period and year. Paper entry forms should be sent with a cheque or postal order (payable to Rockschool Ltd) to the address shown on the entry form. Entry forms sent by post will be acknowledged either by letter or email, while all entries made online will automatically be acknowledged by email.

- Applications received after the expiry of the closing date, whether made by post or online, may be accepted subject to the payment of a late fee.

- Rockschool will allocate your exam to a specific centre and you will receive notification of the exam showing a date, location and time, as well as advice on what to bring to the centre. We endeavour to give you four weeks notice ahead of your exam date.

- You should inform Rockschool of any cancellations or alterations to the schedule as soon as you can because it may not be possible to transfer entries from one centre, or one period, to another without the payment of an additional fee.

- Please bring your music book and CD to the exam. You may use photocopied music if this helps you avoid awkward page turns. The examiner will sign each book during each examination. Please note, you may be barred from taking an exam if you use someone else's music.

- You should aim to arrive for your exam 15 minutes before the time stated on the schedule. Guitarists and bass players should get ready to enter the exam room by taking their instrument from its case and tuning up. This will help with the smooth running of each exam day.

- Each Grade 4 exam is scheduled to last 25 minutes. You can use a small proportion of this time to set up and check the sound levels.

- You will receive a copy of the examiner's marksheet two to three weeks after the exam. If you have passed you will also receive a Rockschool certificate of achievement.

# Bass Grade 4 Marking Schemes

| ELEMENT | PASS | MERIT | DISTINCTION |
|---|---|---|---|
| Performance Piece 1 | 12–14 out of 20 | 15–17 out of 20 | 18+ out of 20 |
| Performance Piece 2 | 12–14 out of 20 | 15–17 out of 20 | 18+ out of 20 |
| Performance Piece 3 | 12–14 out of 20 | 15–17 out of 20 | 18+ out of 20 |
| Technical Exercises | 9–10 out of 15 | 11–12 out of 15 | 13+ out of 15 |
| *Either* Sight Reading *or* Improvisation & Interpretation | 6 out of 10 | 7–8 out of 10 | 9+ out of 10 |
| Ear Tests | 6 out of 10 | 7–8 out of 10 | 9+ out of 10 |
| General Musicianship Questions | 3 out of 5 | 4 out of 5 | 5 out of 5 |
| TOTAL MARKS | 60%+ | 74%+ | 90%+ |

## Performance Certificates | Grades 1–8

| ELEMENT | PASS | MERIT | DISTINCTION |
|---|---|---|---|
| Performance Piece 1 | 12–14 out of 20 | 15–17 out of 20 | 18+ out of 20 |
| Performance Piece 2 | 12–14 out of 20 | 15–17 out of 20 | 18+ out of 20 |
| Performance Piece 3 | 12–14 out of 20 | 15–17 out of 20 | 18+ out of 20 |
| Performance Piece 4 | 12–14 out of 20 | 15–17 out of 20 | 18+ out of 20 |
| Performance Piece 5 | 12–14 out of 20 | 15–17 out of 20 | 18+ out of 20 |
| TOTAL MARKS | 60%+ | 75%+ | 90%+ |

# Bass Guitar Notation Explained

**THE MUSICAL STAVE** shows pitches and rhythms and is divided by lines into bars. Pitches are named after the first seven letters of the alphabet.

**TABLATURE** graphically represents the bass guitar fingerboard. Each horizontal line represents a string, and each number represents a fret.

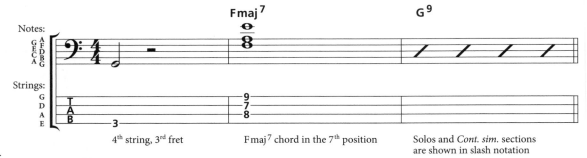

4th string, 3rd fret     Fmaj7 chord in the 7th position     Solos and *Cont. sim.* sections are shown in slash notation

## Definitions For Special Bass Guitar Notation

**HAMMER ON:** Pick the lower note, then sound the higher note by fretting it without picking.

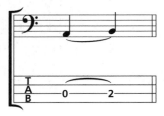

**PULL OFF:** Pick the higher note then sound the lower note by lifting the finger without picking.

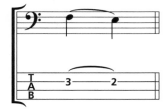

**SLIDE:** Pick the first note and slide to the next. If the line connects (as below) the second note *is not* repicked.

**GLISSANDO:** Slide off of a note at the end of its rhythmic value. The note that follows *is* repicked.

**SLAP STYLE:** Slap bass technique is indicated through the letters **T** (thumb) and **P** (pull).

**TAPPING:** Sound note by tapping the string – circles denote a picking hand tap, squares a fretting hand tap.

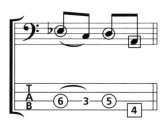

**DEAD (GHOST) NOTES:** Pick the string while the note is muted with the fretting hand.

**NATURAL HARMONICS:** Lightly touch the string above the indicated fret then pick to sound a harmonic.

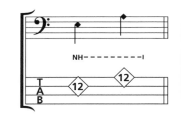

 (accent) ▪ Accentuate note (play it louder).

 (staccato) ▪ Shorten time value of note.

 ▪ Fermata (Pause)

**D.%. al Coda** ▪ Go back to the sign (%), then play until the bar marked **To Coda ⊕** then skip to the section marked ⊕ **Coda**.

**D.C. al Fine** ▪ Go back to the beginning of the song and play until the bar marked **Fine** (end).

 ▪ Repeat bars between signs.

 ▪ When a repeated section has different endings, play the first ending only the first time and the second ending only the second time.

SONG TITLE: ROLLIN'

GENRE: BLUES ROCK

TEMPO: 107 BPM

KEY: B MINOR

TECH FEATURES: SYNCOPATED PHRASES
SOLOING
TIGHT UNISON PHRASES

COMPOSER: STUART RYAN, HENRY THOMAS
& NOAM LEDERMAN

PERSONNEL: STUART RYAN (GTR)
HENRY THOMAS (BASS)
NOAM LEDERMAN (DRUMS)
ROSS STANLEY (KEYS)

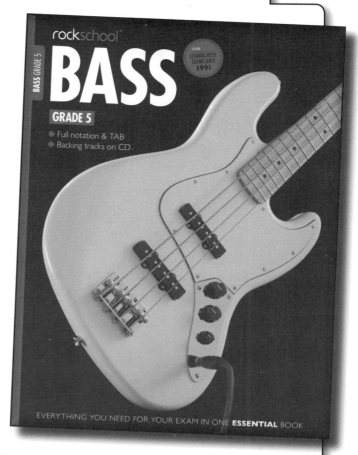

## OVERVIEW

'Rollin'' is a blues rock track akin to the style of contemporary blues guitarist John Mayer. The bassline heard on this piece is a funk-influenced, syncopated line that provides the perfect foundation for the guitar driven elements. There is the opportunity to solo over the chord changes and some unison riffs to play with the guitar, both of which are common elements in modern blues rock.

## STYLE FOCUS

Contemporary blues rock builds on the foundations of the genre laid over the last 30 years by The Jimi Hendrix Experience, Cream, Stevie Ray Vaughan (SRV) and others. The guitar-led style typically features a power trio line-up of guitar, bass and drums, occasionally augmented by a Hammond organ or keys player. The power trio format is favoured by Mayer, an excellent songwriter as well as a guitarist, who has achieved success in this genre.

## THE BIGGER PICTURE

The blues rock genre emerged in Britain in the 1960s when groups like John Mayall's Blues

Breakers, Cream and Fleetwood Mac turned up the distortion on their guitars and performed extended improvisations. The genre remained popular through the 1970s and 1980s thanks to figures such as SRV and Gary Moore.

John Mayer, Derek Trucks and Joe Bonamassa (and their respective groups) keep blues rock alive today.

Many bass players have produced inspirational performances in this genre, including Jack Bruce (Cream), Tommy Shannon (SRV) and, more recently, Pino Palladino who regularly performs with the John Mayer Trio. Palladino, a top session player from Britain, has enjoyed a varied career over the last 30 years from synth-like fretless grooves with 1980s chart-toppers including Paul Young to smooth hip hop grooves with D'Angelo, stadium rock with The Who and now funk-tinged blues rock with Mayer.

## RECOMMENDED LISTENING

While there is a wealth of blues rock from the 20th century, exploring contemporary blues rock is worthwhile, starting with John Mayer's *Continuum* (2006), *Battle Studies* (2009) and the live John Mayer Trio album *Try!* (2005), particularly the tracks 'Who Did You Think I Was?' and 'Wait Until Tomorrow'.

# Rollin' (Grade 5 Preview)

Stuart Ryan, Henry Thomas & Noam Lederman

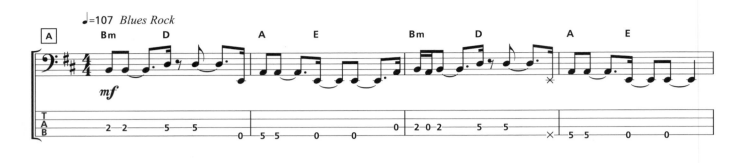

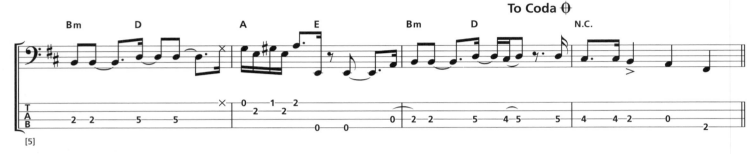

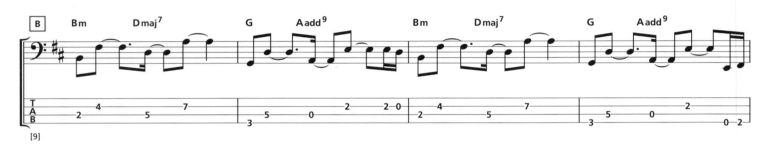

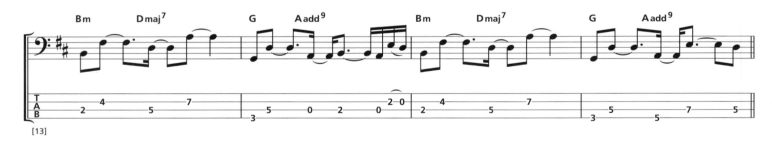

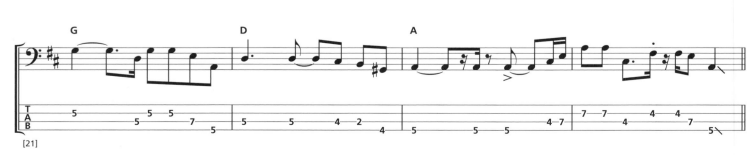

**D** **Bass Solo** (8 bars)

[25]

**Drums Solo** (8 bars)

**E**

[29]

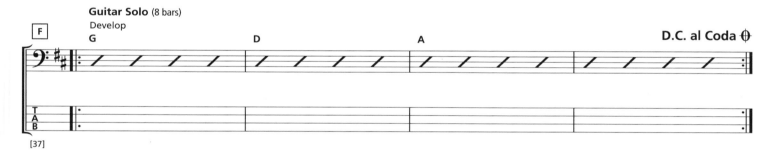

[33]

**Guitar Solo** (8 bars)

**F** Develop

[37]

 **Coda**

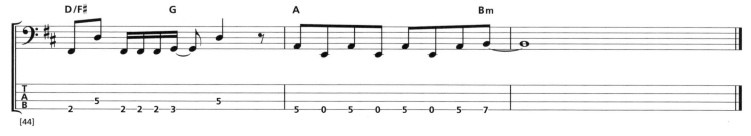

[41]

[44]

# Walkthrough (Grade 5 Preview)

## A Section (Bars 1–8)
This section features a root-based line containing several syncopated figures as well as melodic ideas.

**Bar 6 | *Bass fill***
When playing the bass fill in this bar of 'Rollin' it may help to think of it as an ascending eighth-note line running from G to G# to A (Fig. 1). The G and G# are each followed by an E at the 2nd fret of the D string, where you will be essentially 'filling in the gaps'.

## B Section (Bars 9–16)
This particular section is based around a root-fifth bassline that is syncopated.

**Bars 9–16 | *Root-fifth bassline***
This bassline follows the same rhythmic pattern as the previous section, but uses the root and fifth of each chord instead. The end of each two-bar phrase features two 16th notes that ease the transition to the next chord.

## C Section (Bars 17–24)
This section features a guitar solo, supported by a more active bassline.

**Bars 19–20 | *Fingering***
These two bars can be played far more simply through the use of some careful finger choices (Fig. 2).

## D Section (Bars 25–28)
The D section is the bass solo and your opportunity to improvise a solo line over the chord changes.

**Bars 25–28 | *Improvising a solo***
When working on solo ideas for this part, you should find that the D major scale and D major pentatonic scale work well. You may also like to make a note of the chord tones for each chord and aim to focus your ideas around those where possible. Remember to start with simple, melodic ideas and build from there.

## E Section (Bars 29–36)
This part of the song contains some syncopated accents played with the guitar. Rhythmic accuracy is especially important in this section.

**Bar 29 | *Rhythms***
The rhythm on beat one of this bar is played as two 16th notes followed by an eighth note. The two notes that follow this rhythm are played on the upbeats of beats two and three.

This offbeat rhythm on beats two and three is reused several times in this section.

## F Section (Bars 37–40)
This is another guitar solo and another opportunity for you to improvise your own part – this time a suitable accompaniment part.

**Bars 37–40 | *Improvising an accompaniment***
You should create your own part here. You are free to play as you wish but remember to create a part that is in keeping with the piece. This section features the same chord progression as Section C. You should find that the corresponding major pentatonic scale for each chord will provide appropriate sounding source material.

## G Section (Bars 42–46)
This final section of the song is based around another unison riff that is played with the guitar.

**Bar 42 | *Riff***
When playing the group of 16th notes on beat two, be aware that the last note moves up from an F# to a G. This anticipates the next chord and pushes the line along.

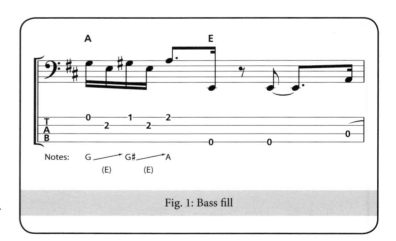

Fig. 1: Bass fill

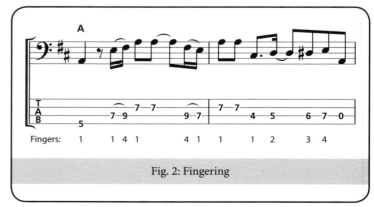

Fig. 2: Fingering

Bass Grade 4